NOV   2013

RESTFUL HOMES

CASAS DE DESCANSO

RÉSIDENCES SECONDAIRES

WOCHENENDHÄUSER

AUTHORS
Fernando de Haro & Omar Fuentes

EDITORIAL DESIGN & PRODUCTION
AM Editores S.A. de C.V.

PROJECT MANAGERS
Valeria Degregorio Vega
Tzacil Cervantes Ortega

COORDINATION
Edali Nuñez Daniel
Martha P. Guerrero Martel

COPYWRITERS
Abraham Orozco
Roxana Villalobos

ENGLISH TRANSLATION
Louis Loizides

FRENCH TRANSLATION
Wordgate Translations

GERMAN TRANSLATION
Heike Ruttkowski

AM EDITORES AM PUBLISHERS

100+ TIPS · IDEAS
restful homes . casas de descanso
résidences secondaires . wochenendhäuser

© 2009, Fernando de Haro & Omar Fuentes
AM Editores S.A. de C.V.
Paseo de Tamarindos 400 B, suite 102, Col. Bosques de las Lomas, C.P. 05120, México, D.F.
Tels. 52(55) 5258 0279, Fax. 52(55) 5258 0556. ame@ameditores.com **www.ameditores.com**

ISBN 13: 978-607-437-023-2

Printed in China.

INTRODUCTION
INTRODUCCIÓN
INTRODUCTION
EINLEITUNG

Building a house in the country means facing challenges that architects and builders alike need to address, such as topography, weather conditions, distances, roads, the supply of materials, services and other factors. At the same time, people are increasingly looking to the countryside to build homes they can rest in and which often become their main or only residence. Here is where they can leave behind the stress and traffic of the cities and breathe in the peace and tranquility of the countryside, the forest, the beach or the mountains. Architects are now setting about the task of devising better solutions for this type of buildings and, as you will see on the following pages, are using the very latest techniques and industrial products to do so. But this does not mean they overlook local styles and locally-available materials that have been used for centuries, such as stone and wood. The outcome of all this is modern homes whose style, nevertheless, contains many traditional elements and which are made with great awareness of the natural setting and the customary vocation of the location. But the creators of these buildings also always try to add an original and novel touch to their work. This book will give you some tips to help you find the ideal way to make your country home a place that is comfortable and relaxing, as well as magnificent and stylish.

Construir una casa en el campo, entraña enfrentar algunas dificultades que los arquitectos y constructores deben resolver adecuadamente, como la topografía, el clima, las distancias, las comunicaciones terrestres, el acopio de materiales, los servicios, entre otras. Sin embargo, cada vez es más frecuente que las personas se decidan a construir una casa de descanso, que en ocasiones suele ser la residencia definitiva, donde puedan aislarse de las grandes concentraciones urbanas, el tránsito de vehículos, el ajetreo cotidiano y para ello buscan refugio en el campo, en el bosque, la playa o la montaña. Los arquitectos de hoy en día se han dado a la tarea de encontrar las soluciones más convenientes para ese tipo de construcciones y en ese caso, como se puede observar en las siguientes páginas, no dudan en emplear las nuevas técnicas y los productos industriales de más reciente ingreso en el mercado, al mismo tiempo hacen uso de detalles constructivos típicos de la zona, así como de los materiales que existen en el sitio y que han sido usados históricamente, como la piedra o la madera. El resultado son casas contemporáneas que, sin embargo, guardan en su estilo muchos elementos que evocan edificaciones tradicionales, siempre respetuosas del entorno natural y de la vocación típica de la zona donde se asientan, pero siempre tratando de aportar algún elemento novedoso y original. He aquí algunos tips para encontrar la solución ideal para una casa en el campo, cómoda y relajada, pero al mismo tiempo bella y con estilo.

Faire construire une résidence secondaire sous-entend faire face à quelques difficultés comme, entre autres, celles qui ont rapport avec la topographie des lieux, le climat, les distances, l'infrastructure routière, le transport du matériel, les divers services. Les architectes et les bâtisseurs doivent trouver les solutions appropriées. Il est pourtant de plus en plus fréquent que des gens se décident à faire construire une résidence secondaire qui, parfois, devient leur résidence principale car elle leur donne la possibilité de s'éloigner des grands centres urbains, de ses embouteillages, de sa frénésie quotidienne et de trouver refuge dans le calme de la campagne, de la forêt, de la montagne ou près de la plage. Les architectes d'aujourd'hui se donnent la tâche de trouver les solutions les plus avantageuses pour ce genre de constructions et ils n'hésitent pas pour y parvenir à utiliser les techniques les plus actuelles et les produits industriels les plus récents sur le marché. Pour autant, ils savent ne pas oublier certains détails architecturaux et certains matériaux typiques de la région utilisés depuis fort longtemps comme la pierre ou le bois. Le résultat, ce sont des maisons contemporaines mais avec un style très marqué qui fait penser à des demeures traditionnelles se fondant harmonieusement avec l'environnement naturel et les caractéristiques de la région où elles se situent. Le résultat, ce sont aussi toujours quelques détails novateurs, quelques idées originales.

Der Bau eines Hauses auf dem Land bedeutet für die Architekten und Bauherren, dass sie viele Schwierigkeiten auf geeignete Weise überwinden müssen, wie die Topographie, das Klima, die Entfernungen, die Strassenanbindung, die Versorgung mit Materialien, die Serviceleistungen usw. Trotzdem werden immer häufiger Landhäuser gebaut, die dann später zum Hauptwohnsitz werden, an denen man den Städtekonzentrationen, dem Strassenverkehr und dem täglichen Stress entgehen kann. Zu diesem Zweck wird ein Zufluchtsort auf dem Land, im Wald, am Strand oder in den Bergen gesucht. Die Architekten sehen sich heutzutage der Aufgabe gegenüber gestellt, die günstigsten Lösungen für diese Art von Bauten zu finden. Auf den folgenden Seiten ist zu sehen, dass dabei neue Techniken und Industrieprodukte zum Einsatz kommen, die erst gerade auf dem Markt erschienen sind. Gleichzeitig wird aber auch Gebrauch von baulichen Details gemacht, die typisch für die Zone sind, sowie auch von den Materialien, die an diesem Ort vorkommen und schon immer in diesem Bereich zum Einsatz gekommen sind, wie zum Beispiel Stein oder Holz. Das Ergebnis sind moderne Häuser, die jedoch in ihrem Stil viele Elemente traditioneller Bauten vereinen, wobei stets das natürliche Umfeld respektiert wird, sowie auch die typischen Eigenheiten der Zone, in der gebaut wird; immer wird aber auch versucht etwas Neuheitliches und Originelles anzubringen. Hier werden einige Tipps gegeben, die beim Finden der idealen Lösung in Bezug auf ein Landhaus helfen, wobei Bequemlichkeit und Entspanntheit und gleichzeitig auch Schönheit und Stil gefragt sind.

COUNTRY HOMES
CASAS EN EL CAMPO
MAISONS DE CAMPAGNE
LANDHÄUSER

The range of options for building houses in the countryside is huge. To begin with, the countryside, as a space to live in, automatically implies a certain distance from the big cities. It can be open country or a forest, or set in the mountains or on a hill, as well as on a riverbank or the shore of a lake.

These buildings are sturdy, and easy to clean and maintain. They have more walls than openings to provide protection against changing weather conditions – cool in summer and warm in winter – and are finished with different types of materials, which are chosen precisely because they are in synch with the setting. The orientation is carefully planned, as is the positioning of different items of comfortable and practical furniture for household services, the kitchen, bathroom and bedrooms, where rest-assuring comfort is a must.

Large windows, terraces and balconies are a great way to make the most of the views of the natural surroundings. If the climate is cold enough, a chimney would also be a good idea.

La construcción de casas en el campo abre un espectro muy grande de posibilidades. En primera instancia, el campo, como un espacio para vivir, significa que podemos referirnos a un sitio más o menos alejado de las concentraciones urbanas y puede ser en el campo abierto, en el bosque, en la montaña, en una colina, en la ribera de un río o en la orilla de un lago.

Se trata de edificaciones sólidas, de fácil mantenimiento y conservación, con más muros que vanos que brinden protección contra los cambios climáticos, frescas en el verano y cálidas en invierno; terminadas con diferentes tipos de materiales, que guarden cierta armonía con el lugar; con una adecuada orientación y convenientemente equipadas con muebles cómodos y funcionales, tanto para los servicios como la cocina y los cuartos de baño, como para las habitaciones, que por definición deben ser confortables, propicias para el descanso.

Los grandes ventanales permiten aprovechar las vistas que ofrece el paisaje natural, lo mismo que las terrazas o miradores y, finalmente, si las condiciones del clima así lo exigen, no debe faltar una buena chimenea.

La construction d'une résidence secondaire à la campagne offre un grand nombre de possibilités architecturales. Admettons d'abord que la campagne, en tant qu'espace de vie, fait référence à un lieu plus ou moins éloigné d'une agglomération qui peut se situer sur un terrain nu, dans une forêt, en montagne, en haut d'une colline ou au bord d'un fleuve ou d'un lac.

Cela signifie aussi que l'on parle de constructions robustes faciles à entretenir et à conserver avec plus de murs que d'espaces ouverts pour résister aux changements climatiques et qui donnent de la fraicheur en été et de la chaleur en hiver. Ce sont aussi des bâtisses construites avec différents matériaux, plutôt en harmonie avec les lieux, orientées avec soin, meublées de façon commode et fonctionnelle tant en ce qui concerne la cuisine et les salles de bain que les chambres qui se doivent d'être confortables et idéales pour se reposer.

Les grandes baies vitrées, tout comme les terrasses ou les balcons, sont nécessaires pour profiter du paysage naturel. Enfin, une bonne cheminée n'est pas superflue si les conditions climatiques l'exigent.

Der Bau von Landhäusern kann auf sehr vielfältige Art und Weise geschehen. In erster Linie bedeutet das Land als Lebensraum, dass es sich um einen Ort handelt, der sich mehr oder weniger fern ab von der Stadt befindet. Es kann sich dabei um ein weites Feld, einen Wald, einen Berg, einen Hügel, das Ufer eines Flusses oder eines Sees handeln.

Es sind solide Bauten zu schaffen, die leicht instandzuhalten sind und mehr Mauern als Öffnungen aufweisen, um uns so vor den klimatischen Einflüssen zu schützen; im Sommer sollen sie kühl sein und im Winter warm. Sie werden mit verschiedenen Materialtypen gefertigt, die auf bestimmte Weise mit der Umgebung harmonieren; mit einer angemessenen Ausrichtung und bequemen und praktischen Möbeln, sowohl in den Servicebereichen, der Küche und den Badezimmern, als auch in den Schlafzimmern, die natürlich besonders angenehm ausgestattet sein sollten, um so eine angemessene Erholung sicherzustellen.

Grosse Fenster ermöglichen es, die natürliche Landschaft zu geniessen, so wie dies auch bei Terrassen und Balkonen der Fall ist. Und wenn die klimatischen Bedingungen dies so erfordern, sollte ein offener Kamin nicht fehlen.

THE HOUSE OF HAMMOCKS
CASA LAS HAMACAS
LA MAISON DES HAMACS
HAUS MIT HÄNGEMATTEN

TIPS - ASTUCES - TIPPS
- The swimming pool visually stretches out towards the lake across the surface of the water at ground level.
- Provoca la extensión visual entre tu alberca y un lago planeando el agua a ras.
- Un lac avec de l'eau à ras bord près de votre piscine agrandit le panorama.
- Wird das Wasser des Schwimmbades bis zum Rand geplant, kann so eine optische Verlängerung zwischen diesem Bereich und dem See erzielt werden.

The landscape
stretches the house
out towards infinity.

Le paysage multiplie
à l'infini l'espace de
la maison.

El paisaje multiplica
al infinito la extensión
de la casa.

Die Landschaft
verlängert die
Ausdehnung des
Hauses ins
Unendliche.

Wood offers many expressive options for covering floors or walls.

La madera adquiere muchas formas de expresión ya sea en los pisos o en los muros como recubrimiento.

Les expressions du bois sont multiples sur le sol comme en tant que revêtement mural.

Holz ermöglicht viele Audrucksformen, gleichgültig ob als Bodenbelag oder Wandbeschlag.

TIPS - ASTUCES - TIPPS
- *Rooftop gardens are an excellent way of blending the material world with the surrounding landscape.*
- *Incluye pérgolas en áreas exteriores intentando armonizar su materialidad con el paisaje.*
- *Utilisez des pergolas à l'extérieur en essayant d'harmoniser leurs matériaux avec ceux du paysage.*
- *Werden Pergolas im Aussenbereich eingeplant, sollte deren Material mit der Landschaft im Einklag stehen.*

ORANGE HOUSE
CASA NARANJA
LA MAISON ORANGE
ORANGEFARBENES HAUS

Large volumes and spaciousness are open to nature, and wooden beams generate a warm and comfortable ambience.

Gran volumetría y amplios espacios abiertos a la naturaleza, donde las vigas de madera crean una atmósfera cálida y confortable.

Grande volumétrie, amples espaces ouverts vers la nature avec des poutres en bois qui créent une atmosphère chaude et confortable.

Grosses Volumen und weite Räume, die zur Natur hin geöffnet sind, wo die Holzbalken eine warme und komfortable Atmosphäre schaffen.

TIPS · ASTUCES · TIPPS
- You can use the light and shade interplay generated by outdoor beams to great effect.
- Aprovecha los efectos de luz y sombra que surgen de la viguería exterior.
- Profitez des effets de l'ombre et de la lumière générés pas les poutres extérieures.
- Nutze die Licht und Schatten-Effekte, die durch Balken im Aussenbereich entstehen.

THE HOUSE OF THE BLINDS
CASA LAS PERSIANAS
LA MAISON AUX STORES
HAUS MIT JALOUSIEN

TIPS - ASTUCES - TIPPS
- *The countryside demands that views be afforded privileged status, and this should be taken into account upon planning how tall your house will be.*
- *El campo obliga a privilegiar las vistas, conviene que lo consideres al planear la altura de tu casa.*
- *La campagne vous oblige à faire attention à la vue. Il est recommandé d'y penser lorsque vous choisirez la hauteur de votre maison.*
- *Auf dem Land ist dem Ausblick besondere Aufmerksamkeit zu schenken, daher ist dieser Punkt auch bei der Planung der Höhe des Hauses zu berücksichtigen.*

Decorative details and contrasting textures can be used to create different moods in the same area.

Grâce à des accessoires décoratifs et des contrastes sur les tissus, on crée des ambiances différentes dans un même lieu.

Mediante elementos decorativos o cambios de texturas se obtienen diferentes ambientes en un mismo espacio.

Durch die Verwendung von dekorativen Elementen oder unterschiedlichen Texturen werden vielfältige Atmosphären im selben Raum geschaffen.

HOUSE OF THE LIGHT
CASA DE LA LUZ
LA MAISON DE LA LUMIÈRE
HAUS MIT LICHT

A sturdy traditional country house.

La solidez de una casa de campo tradicional.

La solidité d'une maison de campagne traditionnelle.

Die Solidität eines traditionellen Landhauses.

A spacious balcony joins the freshness and fragrances of the forest with the top floor bedrooms.

Une ample terrasse qui fait saillie laisse entrer la fraicheur et les parfums de la forêt dans les chambres à l'étage.

Una amplia terraza en voladizo, incorpora la frescura y el aroma del bosque a las habitaciones de la planta superior.

Eine grosse Balkonterrasse lässt die Frische und das Aroma des Waldes in die Räume des oberen Stockwerkes.

SUNSET HOUSE
CASA EL SERENO
LA MAISON PAISIBLE
RUHIGES HAUS

TIPS - ASTUCES - TIPPS
- *The greater the use of natural elements in country homes, the more harmonious the design.*
- *En el campo, cuanto más repitas los elementos naturales, tanto más armonioso será el diseño.*
- *A la campagne, plus les éléments naturels sont déclinés, plus le design de l'ensemble sera harmonieux.*
- *Auf dem Land wird ein umso harmonischeres Design erzielt, je mehr die natürlichen Elemente wiederholt werden.*

TIPS - ASTUCES - TIPPS
- *A comfortable item of furniture or hammock on your terrace will allow you to enjoy the view and relax.*
- *Integra en tu terraza un mueble cómodo o una hamaca, gozarás de la vista y te relajarás.*
- *Placez sur votre terrasse un meuble confortable ou un hamac et vous profiterez de la vue tout en vous relaxant.*
- *Wird ein bequemes Möbel oder eine Hängematte auf der Terrasse angebracht, kann die Sicht genossen und entspannt werden.*

Large windows
turn the
surrounding
landscape into
another indoor
decoration option.

Los grandes
ventanales
incorporan la vista
del paisaje como
otro elemento de
la decoración
interior.

Avec les grandes
baies vitrées, le
paysage devient
un autre élément
de la décoration
intérieure.

Die grossen Fenster
beziehen den Blick
auf die Landschaft
als ein weiteres
Element der
Innendekoration
mit ein.

THE TERRACE
LA TERRAZA
LA TERRASSE
DIE TERRASSE

This highly versatile area can be turned into a living room and visually brings together the inside and the outside.

Espacio muy versátil, una terraza que se convierte en sala de estar y comunica visualmente el interior y el exterior.

Espace polyvalent, une terrasse se transforme en salon et dégage la vue en mêlant extérieur et intérieur.

Ein sehr vielseitiger Bereich ist eine Terrasse, die sich in das Wohnzimmer verwandelt und visuell sowohl mit dem Innen- als auch mit dem Aussenbereich verbunden ist.

TIPS - ASTUCES - TIPPS

• Try to make the transition between indoors and outdoors as smooth as possible using transparent and natural materials.
• Procura que la transición interior-exterior sea suave usando transparencias y materiales de procedencia natural.
• Atténuez les passages entre l'intérieur et l'extérieur en utilisant des surfaces transparentes et des matériaux d'extraction naturelle.
• Versuche immer, den Übergang von innen nach aussen weich zu gestalten, indem Transparenz und natürliche Materialien zum Einsatz kommen.

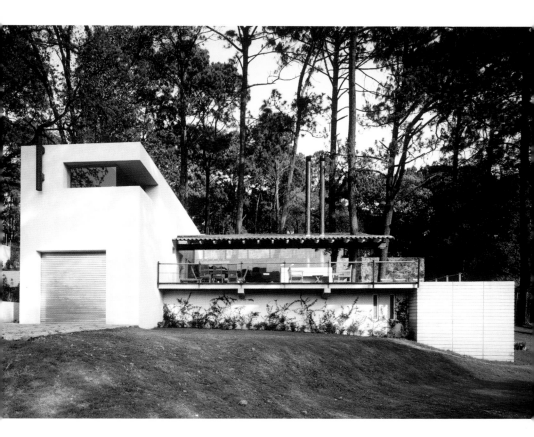

THE TRANQUIL VILLA
VILLA QUIETUD
LA VILLA DE LA QUIÉTUDE
HAUS DER RUHE

This architectural concept affords elegance and comfort for the whole building.

El concepto arquitectónico, de gran carácter, transmite la sensación de comodidad y elegancia a todo el conjunto.

Le concept architectural, très spécifique, donne à l'ensemble de la pièce une atmosphère pratique et élégante.

Das architektonische Konzept hat grossen Charakter und vermittelt den Eindruck von Bequemlichkeit und Eleganz im gesamten Raum.

THE HOUSE OF BEAMS
CASA DE LAS VIGAS
LA MAISON POUTRES
HAUS MIT BALKEN

TIPS - ASTUCES - TIPPS
- *Use easy-to-clean, low maintenance floors if your house is in the country.*
- *Elige pisos de fácil limpieza y bajo mantenimiento si tu casa está en el campo.*
- *Choisissez des sols faciles à nettoyer et à entretenir pour une maison à la campagne.*
- *In einem Landhaus sollten einfach zu reinigende Böden gewählt werden, die wenig Instandhaltung erfordern.*

Large spaces for
the family to spend
time together in.

Des espaces
amples et étendus
conçus pour une
vie familiale en
commun.

Espacios amplios
y extendidos para
la convivencia
familiar.

Grosse und
weite Räume für
das familiäre
Zusammensein.

A house on the shore of a lake, whose architecture and furnishings boast an ideal combination of light, color and textures.

Una casa a la orilla del lago, con una acertada combinación de luz, color y textura en el concepto arquitectónico y el mobiliario.

Une maison au bord du lac et un mélange judicieux de lumière, de couleurs, de tissus associé à un concept architectural et un mobilier élaborés.

Ein Haus am Ufer des Sees mit einer gekonnten Kombination von Licht, Farbe und Textur im Bereich des architektonischen Konzeptes und der Möbel.

TIPS - ASTUCES - TIPPS
- *Earthy colors, wood and natural fibers speak the same language as the natural surroundings.*
- *Colores térreos, madera y fibras naturales conforman un lenguaje afín al entorno natural.*
- *Les associations couleurs terre, bois et fibres naturelles sont en parfaite symbiose avec l'environnement.*
- *Erdfarben, Holz und Naturfasern harmonieren mit der natürlichen Umgebung.*

RED SPACE
ESPACIO ROJO
LA MAISON POURPRE
ROTER BEREICH

White tones convey brightness, while wood evokes different sensations.

Los tonos blancos transmiten luminosidad y la madera provoca distintas sensaciones.

Les tons blancs donnent de la luminosité et le bois provoque des sensations variées.

Die weissen Farbtöne vermitteln Helligkeit und das Holz ruft verschiedene Gefühle hervor.

SEAGULL HOUSE
CASA GAVIOTA
LA MAISON GOËLAND
MÖWEN-HAUS

TIPS - ASTUCES - TIPPS
• A fireplace is ideal for sheer comfort and evoking the ambience of the countryside.
• La chimenea te ayudará a evocar confort y a resguardarte del clima campirano.
• La cheminée vous aidera à faire de l'endroit une demeure confortable et à vous protéger du climat de la campagne.
• Der offene Kamin ruft Bequemlichkeit hervor und schützt vor dem Klima auf dem Lande.

Three great
settings for rest and
contemplation.

Trois atmosphères
différentes propices
au repos et à la
contemplation.

Tres ambientes
ideales para el
descanso y la
contemplación.

Drei ideale
Atmosphären
zum Erholen und
Ausspannen.

THE HOUSE OF THE BIRD
CASA AVE
LA MAISON DES OISEAUX
VOGEL-HAUS

The roof, with its inward slope, resembles the open wings of a bird in flight in the midst of thick forest.

El tejado, con la pendiente invertida, sugiere las alas abiertas de un ave en pleno vuelo, en medio de la espesura del bosque.

Le toit, avec sa pente inversée, nous fait penser aux ailes déployées d'un oiseau en plein vol qui se fond dans l'épaisseur de la forêt.

Das Dach mit der umgekehrten Neigung, erinnert an die geöffnenten Flügel eines Vogels im Flug, inmitten des dichten Waldes.

TIPS - ASTUCES - TIPPS
- *Exposed materials in their natural state are ideal for creating an original façade.*
- *Puedes crear una fachada original utilizando distintos materiales expuestos en su estado original.*
- *En utilisant divers matériaux distincts, bien en vue et à l'état original, vous parviendrez à créer une façade originale.*
- *Eine originelle Fassade kann durch die Verwendung von verschiedenen Materialien in ihrem Naturzustand erzielt werden.*

The double ceiling and glass walls of the building create a feeling of being in open countryside protected by the shade of the trees.

La doble altura y los muros de cristal transmiten la sensación de encontrarse a campo abierto, bajo la sombra protectora de los árboles.

Les deux hauteurs de toit et les vitres en verre nous donnent la sensation d'être en plein air, sous l'ombre protectrice des arbres.

Die doppelte Deckenhöhe und die Glaswände erwecken den Eindruck, sich inmitten der freien Natur zu befinden, im schützenden Schatten der Bäume.

THE HOUSE OF GLASS
CASA DE CRISTAL
LA MAISON DE CRISTAL
GLASHAUS

TIPS - ASTUCES - TIPPS
- *Immerse yourself in the very depths of the forest using the protective and transparent qualities of glass.*
- *Rodéate del bosque circundante aprovechando la protección y transparencia que brinda el vidrio.*
- *Profitez du bois aux alentours grâce à la transparence et à la protection du verre.*
- *Umgib dich mit Wald, indem der Schutz und die Transparenz von Glas genutzt wird.*

LEEWARD
SOTAVENTO
EN PLEIN VENT
WINDSCHATTEN

TIPS - ASTUCES - TIPPS
- *The textures of the home's building materials can be brought out with lighting that sweeps upwards and downwards.*
- *Resalta con luz rasante ascendente y descendente la textura de los materiales constructivos.*
- *La lumière rasante ascendante et plongeante met en valeur la texture des matériaux de la construction.*
- *Hebe mit auf- und absteigendem Licht die Textur der Baumaterialien hervor.*

The shapes of
the fine wood
soffit bring a
performance of
light and shade
to life during the
course of the day.

Un jeu entre
ombres et lumières
tout le long du jour
pour mettre en
valeur le plafond
en bois fins.

Juego de luces y
sombras a lo largo
del día creados
por las formas del
plafón de maderas
finas.

Licht- und
Schattenspiel im
Verlauf des Tages
aufgrund der Decke
mit Balken aus
Edelholz.

This steel and glass building rests on pilings to allow it float harmoniously above the uneven terrain.

Une structure en acier et en verre, soutenue par des piliers, et la maison épouse les irrégularités du terrain sur lequel elle est construite.

Una estructura de acero y cristal, asentada sobre pilotes, logra que la casa flote libremente sobre las irregularidades del terreno.

Eine Struktur aus Stahl und Glas auf Pfählen führt dazu, dass das Haus frei auf dem ungleichmässigen Grundstück schwebt.

THE STABLES
LAS CABALLERIZAS
LES ÉCURIES
DIE STALLUNGEN

TIPS - ASTUCES - TIPPS
- *If the house is to be built on a downward slope, try to locate it at the top to make the most of the view afforded by this vantage point.*
- *En topografías descendentes procura construir en la parte más alta y privilegiar las vistas desde alturas.*
- *Il est préférable de placer sa maison au plus haut d'un terrain en pente pour profiter de la vue la plus élevée.*
- *Bei abfallender Topographie sollte auf der höchsten Stelle gebaut werden, denn so kann die Aussicht von oben herab genutzt werden.*

TIPS - ASTUCES - TIPPS
- For the daring only, a great contrast can be achieved by architecture based on glass and metal in a natural setting.
- Atrévete a contrastar los elementos del entorno natural con una arquitectura basada en vidrio y metal.
- N'hésitez pas à opposer les éléments naturels de l'endroit à une architecture basée sur le verre et le métal.
- Schaffe einen Kontrast zu den Elementen der natürlichen Umgebung, indem eine Architektur auf der Basis von Glas und Metall zum Einsatz kommt.

PANORAMIC HOUSE
CASA PANORÁMICA
LA MAISON BELVÉDÈRE
HAUS MIT PANORAMABLICK

TIPS - ASTUCES - TIPPS

- *Harness the full splendor of the trees that stand next to your home by incorporating them into the architecture but affording them the space they need.*
- *Explota la belleza de los árboles más cercanos a tu edificación integrándolos pero dejándoles su espacio.*
- *Profitez de la beauté des arbres les plus proches de votre propriété en les intégrant à votre projet mais en leur laissant leur propre espace.*
- *Nutze die Schönheit der Bäume in der Nähe des Hauses und beziehe sie mit ein, wobei ihnen gleichzeitg aber auch Platz gelassen werden sollte.*

Bright light brings
out the textures.

Une luminosité
brillante pour
accentuer l'effet
des textures.

Brillante
luminosidad
que acentúa las
texturas.

Durch den grossen
Lichteinfall werden
die Texturen
hervorgehoben.

THE HIDDEN ABODE
LA ESCONDIDA
LA MAISON CACHÉE
VERSTECKTES HAUS

A haven of peace
set in the forest.

Un remanso de
paz en el terreno
silvestre.

Un havre de paix
en pleine forêt.

Ein stilles
Plätzchen auf
einem verwegenen
Grundstück.

TIPS - ASTUCES - TIPPS
- Mimic the surroundings with the outside of the house, while using the inside to stamp your own hallmark.
- Hacia el exterior conviene mimetizarte con el paisaje, mostrando más tu toque en el decorado al interior.
- Pour l'extérieur, il convient de se fondre avec le paysage. Il vaut mieux réserver ses goûts pour la décoration de l'intérieur.
- Nach aussen ist es angebracht, sich mit der Landschaft zu tarnen, wodurch der persönliche Touch der Innendekoration noch stärker zur Geltung kommt.

The sharply sloping wooden roof opens up a large window to take in the full splendor of the lakeside setting.

La pente fortement inclinée d'un toit traditionnel avec dessous une grande baie vitrée pour profiter de la vue magistrale sur le lac.

La pronunciada pendiente del tejado rústico, deja abierto un gran ventanal por donde entra la majestuosidad del paisaje lacustre.

Das steile, rustikale Dach verfügt über ein grosses Fenster, durch das die schöne Seelandschaft zu sehen ist.

THE HOUSE BY THE LAKE
CASA DEL LAGO
LA MAISON DU LAC
HAUS AM SEE

THE MURMURING HOUSE
CASA RUMOROSA
LA MAISON DES MURMURES
RAUSCHENDES HAUS

Large elements enriched by artistic and decorative touches.

Grandes volúmenes enriquecidos por el arte y la decoración.

Des espaces très grands enrichis par des objets d'art et par la décoration.

Grosse Ebenen, die mit Kunst und Dekoration berreichert wurden.

This two-floor architectural project, with its very modern details, blends into the surrounding landscape perfectly.

El proyecto arquitectónico, con detalles de gran modernidad en su doble altura, se integra perfectamente al paisaje.

Un projet architectural avec ses deux hauteurs de toit aux détails modernes qui se fond parfaitement dans le paysage.

Das architektonische Projekt, das eine doppelte Deckenhöhe und sehr moderne Details aufweist, fügt sich perfekt in die Landschaft ein.

THE HOUSE OF ROOF TILES
LA CASA DE LOS TEJADOS
LA MAISON AUX TUILES
HAUS DER VIELEN DÄCHER

TIPS - ASTUCES - TIPPS
- For hot rainy climates, a white façade and tiled roofs are the best bet.
- Escoge una fachada blanca y techos de teja para ambientes campiranos calurosos y lluviosos.
- Pour une atmosphère rurale caractérisée par de la chaleur et de la pluie, optez pour une façade blanche et un toit en tuile.
- Wähle eine weisse Fassade und Dächer mit Dachpfannen, um eine warme und regnerische Landatmosphäre zu schaffen.

THE YELLOW WALL
MURO AMARILLO
UN MUR OCRE
GELBE WAND

This expression
of pure geometry
is man's reply to
nature.

Un ejercicio de
geometría pura
como respuesta
del hombre frente
a la naturaleza.

La réponse de
l'être humain
face à la nature:
un exercice de
géométrie pure.

Eine reine
Geometrie als
Antwort auf die
Begegnung von
Mensch und Natur.

BEACH HOMES
CASAS EN LA PLAYA
VILLAS DE BORD DE MER
STRANDHÄUSER

The outcome of any coastal project will depend on the setting, not just because it acts as a frame for the architecture itself, but because it includes the presence of natural factors such as very hot weather, humidity, land conditions, the type of materials available and the behavior of other phenomena.

Beach homes necessarily blend in with the environment without altering it. This is why locally available materials such as palm leaves for roofing, trunks in their natural state and wood for consoles are used together with large windows, open spaces, high roofs, stone floors, circular structures, as well as terraces and living areas open to the caress of the sea breeze but protected from harsh weather conditions.

Architectural styles vary from rustic settings to pure and sophisticated avant-garde creations, based on sharp lines, continuous planes and dynamic structures for split levels. But the aim is essentially to build a sanctuary, a small personal paradise where the setting can be enjoyed to the full in total comfort and in a peaceful and cozy ambience.

El entorno determina el resultado de cualquier proyecto que se realice en las superficies costeras, no únicamente porque sirve de marco a la arquitectura misma, sino porque implica la presencia de elementos de la naturaleza como el clima excesivamente cálido, la humedad, las condiciones del terreno, el tipo de materiales disponibles y el comportamiento de los fenómenos naturales.

Por su naturaleza, la casa en la playa se incorpora al paisaje sin alterarlo por lo que con mucha frecuencia se recurre a materiales regionales, techos de palma, troncos en estado natural, ménsulas de madera, grandes ventanales, espacios abiertos, techumbres altas, pisos de piedra, estructuras circulares y terrazas y salas de estar expuestas a la acción de las brisas marinas y a salvo de los temporales. El estilo arquitectónico es variado, desde los ambientes rústicos hasta las más depuradas sofisticaciones de la vanguardia; líneas claras y bien definidas, planos continuos o estructuras dinámicas para salvar desniveles, pero todo basado en la premisa de que se pretende crear un refugio, un pequeño paraíso personal donde se disfrute del paisaje, con la máxima comodidad y en una atmósfera apacible y confortable.

Le milieu naturel est déterminant pour tout projet architectural en bord de mer parce que la construction doit s'y fondre mais surtout parce cela sous-entend la présence d'éléments naturels qu'on ne peut ignorer comme un climat très chaud, une humidité prononcée, un terrain particulier, des matériaux pas toujours disponibles et des phénomènes atmosphériques parfois extrêmes. De par sa nature, une villa en bord de mer doit se fondre dans le paysage sans le modifier. C'est pour cette raison que l'on a souvent recours à des matériaux de la région, à des toits de feuilles de palmier, du bois à l'état brut ou non que l'on utilisera par exemple pour les corbeaux, de grandes baies vitrées, des espaces ouverts, une importante hauteur de plafond, des sols de pierre, des structures circulaires ou des terrasses et des pièces communes traversées par les brises marines mais à l'abri des orages. L'architecture employée est variée. Cela va du rustique à l'avant-gardisme le plus sophistiqué et le plus épuré en passant par des lignes claires et bien définies, des plans continus ou des structures dynamiques pour résoudre le problème de la dénivellation. Mais toutes ces idées ne poursuivent qu'un seul objectif : donner naissance à une maison qui servira de refuge, un petit paradis personnel où l'on pourra apprécier le paysage, à la fois pratique, tranquille et confortable.

Die Umgebung ist ausschlaggebend für jedes Projekt, das an der Küste in die Tat umgesetzt wird, und dies nicht nur, weil sie als Rahmen für die Architektur dient, sondern auch, weil natürliche Elemente zu berücksichtigen sind, wie ein ausgesprochen warmes Klima, Feuchtigkeit, die Bedingungen des Grundstückes, die Art von vorhandenen Materialien und das Verhalten der Naturphänomene.
Aufgrund seiner Natur, fügt sich ein Strandhaus in die Landschaft ein, ohne diese zu beeinträchtigen. Aus diesem Grunde werden häufig regionale Materialien verwendet, wie Palmdächer, naturbelassene Stämme, Holzkonsolen, grosse Fenster, offene Räume, hohe Dächer, Steinböden, runde Strukturen und Terrassen sowie Wohnzimmer, die der Meeresbrise ausgesetzt und geschützt vor Wettereinflüssen sind. Der architektonische Stil ist vielfältig, von rustikalen Atmosphären bis hin zu den reinsten avantgardistischen Sophistikationen; klare und eindeutig definierte Linien, endlose Ebenen oder dynamische Strukturen, um Unebenheiten auszugleichen, aber all dies unter der Prämisse, einen Zufluchtsort zu schaffen, ein kleines, persönliches Paradies, in dem die Landschaft genossen werden kann, mit der grösstmöglichen Wohnlichkeit und in einer ruhigen und angenehmen Atmosphäre.

The raised roof has been made with local materials, like the old Caribbean huts, to crown an otherwise modern architectural style with open spaces and sturdy structures.

La alta techumbre, hecha con materiales autóctonos como las antiguas cabañas caribeñas, es el marco para un diseño arquitectónico moderno, de espacios abiertos y estructuras sólidas.

Un toit très haut conçu avec des matériaux traditionnels et qui rappelle les antiques cases des Caraïbes couronne un design architectural moderne avec des espaces ouverts et des structures robustes.

Das hohe Dach, das aus originalen Materialien der einstigen karibischen Hütten gefertigt wurde, ist ein Zeichen eines modernen, architektonischen Designs mit offenen Bereichen und soliden Strukturen.

THE HUT
CASA BOHÍO
LA VILLA CABANE
BOHÍO-HAUS

TIPS - ASTUCES - TIPPS
• Thatched roofs look great, allow the breeze to pass through and make air conditioning unnecessary.
• Los techos de palapa son lucidores, permiten que el viento corra y evitan el clima artificial.
• Les toits en feuille de palmier ont belle allure, permettent la circulation du vent et l'air conditionné est inutile.
• Die Dächer über der Terrasse am Strand sehen wunderschön aus und ermöglichen, dass der Wind hindurchstreicht; so wird ein künstliches Klima vermieden.

THE WATER ALLEY
CALLEJÓN DE AGUA
LA VILLA AUX CANAUX
WASSERGASSE

The swimming pool, with its generous aqueous spread, comes across as both an indoor space and an outdoor one in this minimalist house.

La piscina, como una generosa alfombra de agua, se concibe tanto como un espacio exterior como interior de la casa.

La piscine, tel un long tapis aquatique, est un lieu à la fois extérieur et intérieur pour cette villa minimaliste.

Das Schwimmbad erweckt den Eindruck eines grossen Teppiches aus Wasser und kann sowohl aus dem Äusseren als auch aus dem Inneren des Hauses im minimalistischen Stil wahrgenommen werden.

TIPS - ASTUCES - TIPPS

• *Make the most of the available space by pointing the rafters towards the surrounding landscape.*

• *Aprovecha la profundidad del espacio apuntando dinámicamente con vigas hacia el entorno.*

• *Profitez avec dynamisme de la profondeur de l'espace en le mettant en valeur avec des poutres.*

• *Nutze die Tiefe des Raumes, indem die Balken in Richtung Umgebung zeigen.*

THE HOUSE OF BAMBOO
CASA LOS BAMBÚS
LA MAISON DE BAMBOU
BAMBUS-HAUS

TIPS - ASTUCES - TIPPS
- *Semicircles in the interior design will oblige the furniture to follow its contours.*
- *Si incluyes semi-círculos en el diseño interior provoca que los muebles sigan la forma.*
- *Si vous pensez à des demi-cercles pour la décoration intérieure, choisissez des meubles qui en épousent la forme.*
- *Werden Halbkreise mit in das Innendesign einbezogen, sollten auch die Möbel dieser Form folgen.*

The curved façade describes a perfect circle with the sweep of the terrace facing the scenery.

El muro curvo de la fachada forma un círculo perfecto con el movimiento de la terraza que mira al paisaje.

Le mur incurvé de la façade forme un cercle parfait en accord avec la terrasse ouverte sur le paysage.

Die kurvige Mauer der Fassade bildet einen perfekten Kreis mit der Form der Terrasse, die den Blick auf die Landschaft ermöglicht.

THE HOUSE OF THE ROCKS
CASA LAS ROCAS
LA VILLA DU ROCHER
FELSEN-HAUS

The architectural concept seems to have been conceived from some large rocks sitting in front of the house.

El concepto arquitectónico parece haber nacido de la enorme roca al pie de la casa.

L'énorme rochers aux pieds de la villa semblent avoir donné naissance à sa conception architecturale.

Das architektonische Konzept scheint seinen Ursprung bei dem grossen Felsen am Fuss des Hauses zu haben.

THE HOUSE OF THE ROTUNDA
CASA DE LA ROTONDA
LA VILLA DE LA ROTONDE
ROTUNDEN-HAUS

This house really makes the most of the available views, with its main façade facing the forest and a spacious terrace topped by a palm roof looking out to sea.

La casa obtiene el máximo provecho de las vistas, la fachada principal mira hacia el bosque y una terraza de amplias dimensiones y techo de palma voltea hacia el mar.

Une villa où l'on profite au maximum de la vue avec une façade principale qui donne sur la forêt, une terrasse très ample et un toit en feuilles de palmier face à la mer.

Dieses Haus hat den Ausblick so gut wie eben nur möglich genutzt, denn die Hauptfassade ist zum Wald hin gerichtet und die grossangelegte Terrasse mit Palmdach ermöglicht den Blick aufs Meer.

TIPS - ASTUCES - TIPPS
- A good way to create a comfortable ambience indoors is by using thick white walls and sloped ceilings.
- Con muros gruesos y blancos y techos inclinados conseguirás un ambiente interno confortable.
- D'épais murs blancs et des toits inclinés souligneront le confort intérieur de la pièce.
- Sind dicke, weisse Mauern und geneigte Dächer vorhanden, entsteht eine bequeme Atmosphäre im Inneren.

VILLA ZERO
VILLA CERO
LA VILLA ZÉRO
VILLA NULL

TIPS - ASTUCES - TIPPS

- *The natural color of plants can provide a very good contrast with the tone of the walls.*
- *Aprovecha el color natural de las plantas haciéndolo contrastar con el tono de muros.*
- *Utilisez la couleur naturelle des plantes en l'opposant au ton des murs.*
- *Nutze den Naturton der Pflanzen und lasse ihn mit dem Farbton der Wände kontrastieren.*

The sturdy wooden structure of the double height roof crowns the common areas of the house with plenty of space and no inner walls.

La solide structure en bois du toit à double hauteur couvre amplement et sans murs intérieurs les pièces communes de la villa.

La sólida estructura de madera del techo de doble altura, cubre con amplitud y sin muros interiores, los espacios comunes de la casa.

Die solide Holzstruktur des Daches mit doppelter Deckenhöhe bedeckt grosszügig und ohne Wände im Inneren die Gemeinschaftsbereiche dieses Hauses.

TIPS - ASTUCES - TIPPS
- *A rule of thumb in interior design is that you need to find a way of framing the most enchanting views.*
- *Una máxima del diseño es que encuentres la manera de encuadrar las vistas con encanto.*
- *Un atout majeur de tout design : parvenir à encadrer la vue avec talent.*
- *Das schönste Design entsteht, wenn der Ausblick geschmackvoll eingerahmt wird.*

SEA BREEZE
BRISA DEL MAR
BRISE MARINE
MEERESBRISE

The pool reflects the textures and vibrant colors of the wall, adding a dash of sky blue for good measure.

El espejo de la piscina repite la textura y el vivo color del muro y lo complementa con el azul del cielo.

La piscine est un miroir qui reflète la texture et la teinte vive du mur et le colore avec le bleu du ciel.

Das Spiegelbild des Schwimmbades reflektiert die Textur und die lebendige Farbe der Mauer, wobei dies durch die blaue Farbe des Himmels ergänzt wird.

TIPS - ASTUCES - TIPPS

• Doors and windows made with wooden slats are a very functional option for beach homes.

• Las puertas y ventanas con rejilla de madera te serán funcionales en la playa.

• Portes et fenêtres avec une ossature en bois vous seront très utiles sur le littoral.

• Türen und Fenster mit Holzlamellen sind funktionell am Strand.

Soft and subtle
hues, toned by
the effect of the
lighting, generate
a very warm and
intimate ambience.

Las tonalidades
suaves y delicadas,
matizadas por
los efectos de la
iluminación, crean
una atmósfera
íntima de gran
calidez.

Les tons suaves et
délicats nuancés
par les effets
de l'éclairage
apportent à
cette villa une
atmosphère intime
de haute qualité.

Die weichen und
raffinierten Farbtöne,
die durch die
Beleuchtungseffekte
abgetönt werden,
verleihen eine sehr
gemütliche, private
Atmosphäre.

LONE PALM HOUSE
CASA PALMA SOLA
LA VILLA AU PALMIER SOLITAIRE
VERSTECKTES PALMHAUS

The contrasts generated by the water's blue surface join forces with the architecture in this tranquil sanctuary.

Los contrastes en torno a la azulada superficie del agua, se unen a la arquitectura en este refugio de paz.

Le camaieu de bleus de la surface de l'eau sont un des éléments de l'architecture pour ce havre de paix.

Die Kontraste um die blaue Oberfläche des Wassers herum vereinen sich mit der Architektur dieses friedlichen Rückzugsortes.

THE SNAIL HOUSE
CASA CARACOLA
LA VILLA COQUILLAGE
SCHNECKENHAUS

TIPS - ASTUCES - TIPPS
- *Create harmony by incorporating furniture in the architecture and harmonizing the finishes.*
- *Cuando integras muebles a la arquitectura y conjugas sus acabados creas armonía.*
- *Vous créez de l'harmonie en intégrant des meubles avec des finitions choisies à l'architecture.*
- *Werden Möbel in die Architektur mit einbezogen und deren Oberflächenbeschaffung vereinigt, so führt dies zu Harmonie.*

The exquisite architectural work, with rounded edges, blends in perfectly with the rustic finish of the trunk supports.

Un travail architectural très fin avec des bords ronds qui s'harmonisent avec les finitions rustiques et les corbeaux en rondins.

El fino trabajo arquitectónico, con bordes redondeados, armoniza con el acabado rústico de las ménsulas de troncos.

Die edle architektonische Arbeit mit abgerundeten Rändern harmoniert mit der rustikalen Oberfläche der Stämme.

Water flows through a thin channel to a pool at the front of the house before narrowing once again to pursue its route in full view of the wooden enclosure of the overlooking balcony.

L'eau passe par un bassin étroit pour se jeter dans la piscine face à la villa puis resserre son parcours devant le belvédère ceint par une palissade rustique.

El agua corre por un estrecho cauce hasta formar una piscina frente a la fachada y se estrecha nuevamente para seguir su curso frente al mirador de palizadas rústicas.

Das Wasser läuft durch einen engen Kanal, bis es dann in das Schwimmbad gelangt, das sich vor der Fassade befindet und sich dann erneut verengt und bis zum Aussichtspunkt verläuft, der mit rustikalen Palisaden ausgestattet ist.

PALM GROVE HOUSE
CASA PALMARES
LA VILLA DES PALMIERS
PALMEN-HAUS

TIPS - ASTUCES - TIPPS
- If weather conditions allow it, you can create different ecosystems to broaden the scope of the surrounding views.
- Si el clima te lo permite crea distintos ecosistemas para dar versatilidad al paisaje.
- Si le climat le permet, créez plusieurs écosystèmes pour souligner la richesse du paysage.
- Wenn das Klima es erlaubt, sollten verschiedene Ökosysteme geschaffen werden, die die Landschaft vielseitig machen.

SEA POINT HOUSE
CASA PUNTA DEL MAR
LA VILLA DU BORD DE MER
HAUS AN DER MEERESSPITZE

TIPS - ASTUCES - TIPPS
- *Building materials of a similar tone can provide exquisite results.*
- *La incorporación de materiales constructivos con tonalidad similar te permitirá lucir una arquitectura sobria.*
- *Des matériaux de construction tous dans des mêmes tons vous permettront d'envisager un architecture sobre.*
- *Die Verwendung von Baumaterialien mit ähnlichen Farbtönen, führt zu einer schlichten Architektur.*

This terrace with its markedly regional look offers a great vantage point over the surrounding scenery.

Un projet architectural qui préserve le milieu naturel de la région avec cette terrasse qui domine tout le paysage.

El proyecto arquitectónico preserva el ambiente regional en esta terraza que domina la extensión del paisaje.

Dieses architektonische Projekt schützt die Umwelt durch die Terrasse, die die ausgedehnte Landschaft dominiert.

HOUSE ON A CLIFF
CASA DEL RISCO
LA VILLA PARAPET
KLIPPEN-HAUS

A key element of this project is the curved contours of the pool, whose blue tone contrasts with that of the sky and with the colorful range of rich textures inside the house.

La clave del conjunto es el sinuoso perfil de la piscina, revestida de un color azul que contrasta con el cielo y el juego cromático de las ricas texturas del interior.

L'élément-clé est constitué par les bords ondulés de la piscine dont le bleu s'oppose à celui du ciel et à la palette chromatique à base de teintes riches à l'intérieur.

Die Hauptattraktion dieses Komplexes ist die gewundene Form des Schwimmbades, das in einem Blauton gehalten ist, der sich vom Himmel abhebt; die chromatischen Kombinationen der reichhaltigen Texturen im Inneren stehen ebenfalls im Mittelpunkt.

THE SECRET HOUSE
CASA ARCANO
LA VILLA MYSTÈRE
GEHEIMES HAUS

The palm roof seems to melt into the foliage and the architectural shapes adorning the landscape.

La cubierta de palma parece confundirse con el follaje y las formas arquitectónicas que se incorporan al paisaje como elementos decorativos.

La toiture en feuilles de palmier semble faire partie de la végétation naturelle et les formes architecturales se transforment en éléments décoratifs du paysage.

Das Palmdach kann fast mit den umgebenden Blättern verwechselt werden und die archtiektonischen Formen fügen sich wie dekorative Elemente in die Landschaft ein.

TIPS - ASTUCES - TIPPS
- *Make the most of the lay of the land and materials, and your home will blend in with the surroundings.*
- *Explota la topografía y la materialidad y mimetizarás tu casa con el entorno.*
- *Prenez en compte la géographie et les matériaux de la région pour que votre maison se fonde dans l'environnement.*
- *Nutze die Topographie und die Materialien zum Angleich des Hauses an die Umwelt.*

THE HOUSE OF THE TURTLE
CASA DE LA TORTUGA
LA VILLA DE LA TORTUE
SCHILDKRÖTEN-HAUS

TIPS - ASTUCES - TIPPS
- *Take one of your favorite objects and make it the ornamental centerpiece by affording it room to breathe.*
- *Haz de un elemento favorito el centro decorativo dándole respiro en el espacio.*
- *Faites de votre élément favori le centre de la décoration en lui laissant beaucoup d'espace.*
- *Mache ein Lieblingsstück zum Mittelpunkt der Dekoration, so wird dem Raum ein persönlicher Touch verliehen.*

A fresh ambience is created by the combination of wood and finely polished stone items.

L'association de certains éléments en bois avec d'autres en pierre finement polie donne de la fraicheur à l'ensemble.

La combinación de la madera con elementos pétreos finamente pulidos da frescura al ambiente.

Die Kombination von Holz mit edel polierten Steinelementen verleiht der Atmosphäre Frische.

THE HOUSE OF FERNS
CASA DE LOS HELECHOS
LA VILLA FOUGÈRE
HAUS MIT FARN

The building seems to get lost in the surrounding environment. Its most appealing feature is the shapely entrance.

La edificación logra confundirse con el paisaje, pero el punto de atracción es el portón de acceso de forma escultórica.

La bâtisse parvient à se fondre dans le paysage naturel mais l'élément-clé reste la grande porte d'entrée en forme de sculpture.

Das Gebäude fügt sich perfekt in die Landschaft ein, wobei die Hauptattraktion der Eingangsbereich in Form einer Skulptur ist.

THE DOORWAY TO THE SEA
CASA PUERTA AL MAR
LA VILLA PORTE DE LA MER
HAUS MIT TÜR ZUM MEER

The swimming
pool mirrors
the surrounding
vegetation, along
with the rich colors
and textures of the
architecture.

La alberca repite,
como un espejo,
la vegetación
del entorno y la
riqueza cromática
y de texturas de la
arquitectura.

Le bassin, tel
un miroir, reflète
la végétation
environnante
et la richesse
chromatique
et texturale de
l'architecture.

Das Schwimmbad
reflektiert wie
ein Spiegel die
Vegetation der
Umgebung, sowie
die reichhaltige
Chromatik und
die Texturen der
Architektur.

TIPS - ASTUCES - TIPPS
- *The sinewy shapes of nature provide some great options for the architectural design of beach homes.*
- *Considera en el diseño arquitectónico para playa las formas sinuosas de la naturaleza.*
- *Pour le design architectural d'une demeure au bord de la mer, pensez aux formes sinueuses de l'environnement.*
- *Im architektonischen Design am Strand sollten gewundene Formen mit eingeplant werden.*

The solid shapes and intense red tones create a contrast with the delicate blue surface of the sea. At the front of the house, the pool runs parallel to the ocean.

Une solide volumétrie dominée par des teintes rougeâtres très vives s'opposant à la surface bleu pâle de l'océan alors que la limite extérieure rectiligne du bassin vient se heurter à l'océan.

La sólida volumetría, de tono rojizo muy intenso, contrasta con la tenue superficie azulosa del mar, mientras que en el frente el agua de la piscina forma una línea continua con el océano.

Die solide Volumetrie in intensiven Rottönen kontrastiert mit der blauen Oberfläche des Meeres, während vorne das Wasser des Schwimmbades am Horizont in den Ozean übergeht.

THE TRANQUIL BEACH HOUSE
CASA PLAYA QUIETA
LA VILLA DE LA PLAGE PAISIBLE
HAUS AM RUHIGEN STRAND

TIPS - ASTUCES - TIPPS
• If you opt for a lively color for the front of your home, make sure it contrasts well with the surroundings.
• Si decides por un color con personalidad en fachadas busca que contraste con el medio ambiente.
• Si vous vous décidez pour des façades avec des couleurs particulières, faites en sorte qu'elles s'opposent à celles de l'endroit.
• Wenn eine Farbe mit Persönlichkeit für die Fassade gewählt wird, sollte es sich um einen Farbton handeln, der mit der Umwelt kontrastiert.

THE STEEP SLOPE HOUSE
CASA DEL ACANTILADO
LA VILLA DE LA FALAISE
HAUS AN DER FELSWAND

The swimming pool sits on the edge of the slope like a carpet slung outwards from the building.

La piscina, que se asoma al borde del acantilado, parece un tapete que se extiende al pie de la vivienda.

Le bassin qui se termine au bord de la falaise fait penser à un tapis déroulé aux pieds de la construction.

Das Schwimmbad, das über den Rand der Felswand hinausragt, erweckt den Eindruck eines Teppiches, der sich am Fusse des Hauses ausbreitet.

Old trunks have been made into columns, as the centerpiece of the architectural concept.

Los añosos troncos, convertidos en columnas, son punto nodal del concepto arquitectónico.

Les troncs d'arbres séculaires utilisés sous forme de colonnes constituent la base de ce concept architectural.

Die alten Stämme, die als Säulen genutzt wurden, sind der Knotenpunkt des architektonischen Konzeptes.

TIPS - ASTUCES - TIPPS
- *Make the most of natural elements and make them part of the architecture.*
- *Saca ventaja de algunos elementos naturales e intégralos a la arquitectura.*
- *Profitez de quelques éléments naturels et intégrez-les à votre architecture.*
- *Nutze die Vorteile von natürlichen Elementen, indem sie in die Architektur mit einbezogen werden.*

THE HOUSE OF THE HORIZON
CASA DEL HORIZONTE
LA VILLA DES NUAGES
HAUS AM HORIZONT

TIPS - ASTUCES - TIPPS
- You can design terraces on different levels and include overhanging structures.
- Planea tus terrazas en varios niveles y piensa en realizar volados.
- Pensez à une terrasse à plusieurs niveaux et n'oubliez pas les éléments suspendus.
- Plane deine Terrasse auf verschiedenen Ebenen und beziehe auch überstehende Bereiche mit ein.

The poetic outline of this villa overlooking the sea is shaped by beams and pillars made of unpolished wood.

Les poutres et les colonnes en bois brut donnent à cette villa avec vue sur la mer son aspect rustique.

Las vigas y pilares de troncos sin pulir, delinean el carácter bucólico de esta villa con vista al mar.

Die Balken und Pfeiler aus unpolierten Stämmen unterstreichen den bukolischen Charakter dieses Hauses mit Meeresblick.

A large, minimalist living room with a vaulted ceiling culminates with a balcony covered by wooden slats, offering an ideal setting for spending time with the family.

Pour une vie en commun pleine de gaieté, rien de tel qu'une une vaste pièce minimaliste au plafond voûté qui se termine par une terrasse recouverte avec de fines lattes en bois.

Una terraza cubierta con finos listones de madera, es el remate de una larga estancia, de techo abovedado, que ameniza la convivencia familiar.

Eine Terrasse mit einem Dach aus feinen Holzlatten ist der Abschluss des langen Wohnbereiches im Minimalistenstil mit gewölbtem Dach, das das familiäre Zusammensein angenehm macht.

HALF MOON HOUSE
CASA MEDIA LUNA
LA VILLA DEMI LUNE
HALBMOND-HAUS

TIPS - ASTUCES - TIPPS
• *The jacuzzi can be given a lead role in making the lounge and terrace a place of sheer enjoyment.*
• *Convierte al jacuzzi en una parte integral para el disfrute de la estancia y la terraza.*
• *Faites du jacuzzi un élément-clé de la détente et du repos sur la terrasse.*
• *Verwandele den Whirlpool in einen integralen Bestandteil zum Geniessen des Aufenthaltes auf der Terrasse.*

The palm ceiling defines and guides the architectural planes of different areas.

El techo de palma es el hilo conductor de un conjunto de planos arquitectónicos que delimitan diferentes espacios.

Le toit en feuilles de palmier est ici l'élément unificateur de l'ensemble des surfaces cloisonnant diverses pièces.

Das Palmdach ist das Hauptelement der architektonischen Ebenen, die unterschiedliche Bereiche voneinander abgrenzen.

TIPS - ASTUCES - TIPPS
- The combination of terracotta and red wood affords the area a sense of warmth.
- La mixtura de terracotas y maderas rojizas favorece la sensación de calidez espacial.
- Le mélange terracota et bois rouges sont recommandés pour donner une chaleur particulière à l'endroit.
- Die Mischung von Terrakotta und rotem Holz verstärkt den Eindruck von räumlicher Wärme.

architectonic   arquitectónicos   architectoniques   architektonische

84-85 manuel mestre

86-87 ABAX, fernando de haro, jesús fernández,

omar fuentes y bertha figueroa

88-95 - ___ ___

96-97 manuel mestre

98-99 ZOZAYA ARQUITECTOS, enrique zozaya díaz

100-103 marco aldaco

104-105 GRUPO LBC, alfonso lópez baz y

javier calleja

106-109 josé pintado

110-111 ABAX, fernando de haro, jesús

fernández, omar fuentes y bertha figueroa

112-113 DUPUIS, alejandra prieto de palacios

y cecilia prieto de martínez g.

114-119 ABAX, fernando de haro, jesús

fernández, omar fuentes y bertha figueroa

120 mario lazo y CHAVEZ + VIGIL ARQUITECTOS

122-125 ABAX, fernando de haro, jesús

fernández, omar fuentes y bertha figueroa

126-127 manuel mestre

129-131 MARQCÓ, mariangel álvarez c.

y covadonga hernández g.

photographic   fotográficos   photographiques   fotografische

fernando cordero - pgs. 45, 78-81

héctor velasco facio - pgs. 24-25, 36-43, 50-51, 64-69,86-87,104-105, 115, 118-119,129-131

ignacio urquiza - pgs. 34-35,56-57,112-113

jaime navarro - pgs. 20-21

lourdes legorreta - pgs. 22-23,62-63,70

luis gordoa - pgs. 32-33

michael calderwood - pgs. 3-7, 11, 18-19, 26-27, 52(bottom), 54-55,58-61,77, 82-85, 88-103, 106-111,114, 116-117,120-127

paul czitrom - pgs. 28-31, 46-49, 52(top)

Printed in January 2010 in China. Published by AM
Editores S.A. de C.V.
Se terminó de imprimir el mes de enero del 2010 en
China. El cuidado de la edición estuvo a cargo de AM
Editores S.A. de C.V.